Everyday Charisma: Powerhouse Techniques for Mass Appeal, Charm, and Becoming a Social Powerhouse

By Patrick King
Dating and Social Skills coach at
www.PatrickKingConsulting.com

Table of Contents

Everyday Charisma: Powerhouse Techniques for Mass Appeal, Charm, and Becoming a Social Powerhouse

Introduction

I know it's almost a cliché at this point, but there's only been one person who has literally left me speechless from how they carried themselves. He just had that "it" factor, whatever "it" is.

Bill Clinton.

And it's no coincidence that there are literally thousands of stories similar in tenor to mine.

Here's the short version of my experience: he was making an appearance at a community center that was close to where I lived. I wasn't particularly interested in politics at the time, but I **was** interested at the prospect of meeting the President of the United States.

After a rather standard speech about how he commiserated with and related to our community, there was the opportunity for a meet and greet with him. If I was already there and sat through his speech, I figured I might as well take that extra step. At least I could say that I did it, right?

When I got to the front of the line, I mentally reviewed my opinion of the man. He had this everyman public persona that I was sure was fake and put-on – the lovable Arkansas hick. Would I be able to see through him, and would he even make an effort to look me in the eye?

Well, count me wrong.

As just about everyone that met him that day could attest to, he was just a damn likable and charismatic guy. Something about him made you feel like you could grab a beer with him... and when I discovered that he had played his saxophone on Saturday Night Live during his election push, it made me feel like we could be buddies.

Geez, was *that* the power of charisma?

It's hard to describe exactly what he did, but I can describe how he made me feel.

Even when he was surrounded by at least 11 handlers, 12 bodyguards, and countless rabid fans, he made it seem like I was his sole focus. He pretty much ignored everyone else while I was in front of him, made strong eye contact throughout, and asked questions about my life that weren't the normal boring interview questions. He gave me sticky eyes that made it seem like he was engrossed in me.

And what's more – he actually seemed to care about the answers I gave, and asked questions to go deeper! I thought it would be obvious that he would be preoccupied and only there physically, while mentally he was focused on foreign policy or something similar. But he seemed to have genuine fascination with my life. When I said something he agreed with, he nodded his head vigorously and laughed.

Did he really want to know about my dog, family, and favorite class in school?

Probably not, but the empathy he emanated told me otherwise. It kind of sounds like I'm describing an amazing date.

These are traits that most people don't fully utilize in our daily life, but the President of the United States? The singular most powerful person in the western world making such an effort to care? It would be natural to assume that powerful people simply can't be bothered, so accordingly it turns out that presence and warmth are exponentially magnified when displayed from someone powerful.

It just makes you feel good and important, the desired byproducts of charisma.

Much of what creates a feeling of charisma happens in the mind of the recipient, and there are many ways that you can emulate the presence, warmth, and power of a U.S President.

Charisma by itself isn't a quality that is easily defined, but it's easy to define what you want from it and how you want to make others feel because of it.

You want to captivate people, become magnetic, and appear eminently likable and attractive. Others should feel spellbound and transfixed by your presence, yet comfortable and intimate.

This book is a synthesis of the years of intense study, practice, teaching, and observation on the **little** flourishes that charismatic people do differently. Focus on the keyword 'little' – you may be surprised at what has passed you by on a daily basis.

Everyday charisma is how your find your own version of a charismatic presence that makes people stand up and take notice – everyday charisma; huge results!

Chapter 1. Charisma demystified.

Like much of what I write about and teach, charisma is seen by many people to be an immutable quality – meaning that you either have it or you don't, and you can't gain it through by learning or self-improvement.

These are the types of limiting, disorienting beliefs regarding charisma that not only add to its mystique, but also make it hard to develop in your own life.

Thomas the Tank Engine thought he could, and therefore he did. If you don't think you can, then you definitely cannot.

There are so many misconceptions regarding charisma that a lot of people think that they simply don't have what it takes to be charismatic. It's very easy to be intimidated by the whole concept of the effects that a charismatic person can have on people.

But let's break it down and demystify it a bit. Charisma can be defined in any manner of ways, so let's use a manageable and concrete definition.

<u>Charisma: the ability to draw people to you.</u>

That's all. While it's difficult to define exactly what that means, it's easier to say that people will be magnetized towards you and desire your presence.

And just like with any kind of skill, it can be learned.

For ease, charisma can be broken down into different components. These components can then be analyzed, measured, and individually grown.

This book is all about learning how to harness your inner charisma. But the first step of that is to tame the misconceptions and wishful thinking regarding this very powerful human trait.

People want to be charismatic because it opens so many doors. It's very easy to see the career and financial benefits of being charismatic.

Who wouldn't want to meet people and instantly convert them into buyers? Who wouldn't want to walk into a courtroom and easily persuade juries and judges regarding your case? Who wouldn't want to meet people of the opposite sex and get them to like you instantly? Who wouldn't want to be the life of the party?

It's actually this trait's desirability makes it problematic to develop. Charisma is so prized that people think of it as some sort of commodity.

On one hand, you have people who frame it as an almost

quasi-mystical, spiritual, or philosophical terms. It's one of those fleeting human traits that only a select blessed few have.

On the other extreme are people who look at it simply as a means to an end. It's some sort of product that, in their minds, you can buy from a store, check out at the counter, and unpack at home. In their minds, there's really not much difference between being charismatic and following the instructions on a box of instant noodles.

Just like you would unwrap the box of instant noodles, put some hot water and enjoy your meal, in their minds charisma is one of those tools that you just simply need to unpack, understand, and use to your own purpose.

Thankfully, the truth is in between these two extremes. Charisma is neither unattainable and mystical, nor is it some sort of utilitarian commodity. There is a lot of work involved. There is a lot of personal growth that needs to happen for you to truly unleash the power of personal charisma. Of course, that's what makes it so powerful – true everyday charisma embodies a mindset.

If you are charismatic, people will want to be around you. You make them feel special. You give them something that they're missing in their everyday lives.

People who display such strong charisma and such strong force of personality and can almost bend reality. It's as if the rules that apply to most other people don't apply to them. That's how powerful charisma can be.

Reality, for the most part, is man-made. While there is such a thing as the laws of physics and the laws of the natural world, everything else can be modified by sheer human will.

You might not have any grandiose ambitions regarding conquering the world or changing human destiny. But if you want to live a fuller life, if you want to attain more control over your daily set of circumstances, you might want to unleash the power of charisma. It can be harnessed, but it's not a simple checklist that you buy and follow on an almost mechanical or robotic way to tap into.

With that said, if you want to be a positive force, you need to understand charisma and unleash its power in your personal life.

Chapter 2. Living in the here and now.

As I mentioned earlier, one of the reasons charisma is hard to grasp is that people read all sorts of confusing and often conflicting meanings into charisma.

If you ask a hundred people to define charisma, chances are you'll have a hundred different definitions.

But digging deep through those definitions, they tend to center around certain main themes – three key components that always seem to create the desired effect of charisma.

These components are different enough from each other, yet have different enough manifestations that they actually reflect the core components of charisma.

Charisma can be broken down into **presence, power, and warmth**. This chapter will focus on presence.

Presence.

Presence is **not** the feeling of walking into a room and having everyone's head turn to see who you are.

It has nothing to do with what you look like or what you're wearing. It doesn't even have anything to do with the people around you. There are no gimmicks around being present. It's very hard to fake.

The core of presence is simply *how engaged you are* in what's currently happening around you. Be present, live in the moment, and put all the other chatter in your brain on hold. This has a very powerful effect on how you come off to others.

Everybody has the ability to be completely present – all it takes is for you to put your phone into your pocket and really focus on your surroundings. It's not a question of ability; it's a question of desire and awareness. *Do you know the difference this makes, and do you care enough to increase your charisma with it?*

Being present is focusing your full attention on everything that is happening in front of your eyes.

People, your surroundings, and what's being said. Remember that charisma is simply being able to draw people towards you – it's so much easier when you show a true, interrupted interest in someone. They can't help but feel important and that you care, and that's naturally attractive.

The fear of missing out (FOMO) is something that's rampant in society today. It's when you talk to someone, and they can't help but text others or check their social media. This is the opposite of being present, and it can't help but say something about how they perceive you.

When you have FOMO, you naturally disregard what's happening in front of your own face, and that's negative in two ways.

First, you truly miss out on making the most of your time and the best out of any situation. Second, anyone you're with just feels like they are the consolation prize, barely worthy of your attention. It sends the message that you'd rather be somewhere else than in front of them, and that can be borderline insulting and belittling.

Present, charismatic people are intensely curious about the life snapshot they're currently living and whatever is involved in it. They make it an unspoken goal to find out as much as possible about people they are talking to and what makes them tick.

Focus on the here and now.

The first step is to be mentally present.

You'd be surprised as to how many people tend to drift from one day to the other.

If you want to enhance your charismatic presence, you have to immerse yourself in specific moments in time. Be as aware, observant, and present as possible. There is no magic to this, and no tricks.

Realize that your body is a data collection device. You see, smell, hear, taste, touch, and feel things. Emotions, all sorts of interpersonal signals, as well as the ambiance or aura of a particular situation are things that you can detect.

If you want to fine-tune your charismatic presence, a key part of this is heightened sensory perception. Attempting to observe everything around you will make you present whether you want to be or not.

The second step is to be completely comfortable in the present and not think about the future, or what else might be occurring that you are not seeing.

When you're living in the present, you're paying attention to what you see. You're noticing patterns. You allow yourself to really soak up the sight, sound, smells, and the vibrancy and electricity of life happening around you.

We live in a day and age where society teaches us that our happiness is located somewhere in the future. We need to keep planning, and can never turn out brains off because to do so would be detrimental to our ambition and goals. We're all micromanaging our lives to some degree and mentally keeping tabs on what we need to take care of.

This is a shame because it all combines to make us quite uncomfortable in the present and make us feel like we should be doing anything but what we're doing at the moment.

We're always rushing to the future. But once we get closer to that future state, the goal post is always moved several yards forward. It never ends, and you are never actually in the present.

You're like a horse with a carrot dangling in front of it. It doesn't matter how hard you run, you're still the same distance from the carrot.

Of course, focusing on your future is again the opposite of being present.

Tolerate and accept the here and now. Embrace it for what it is — a moment that you will never get back, and that is sorely wasted if you are not present for it.

The charismatic component of presence is a huge part of what draws people to you. It shows others that you are invested in them and care, and is a huge reason of why charismatic folk are so magnetic.

True charisma is connective and all encompassing, and there's only one path to that — being 100% present.

It's in the eyes.

If you want to at least appear more present, you need to look people in the eye when talking to them.

A lot of people talk, but they really are not talking to or hearing each other. They're talking to what that person represents. They just talk and wait for their turn to speak while pretending to listen, not bothering to truly hone in and listen to the other person. In other words, it's all about you.

As Machiavellian as this sounds, this is how most people

treat each other these days.

When you look at somebody in the eye, you are giving yourself the opportunity to truly see that person as a person who is worth understanding and accepting on their own terms.

Not only are you able to understand people better, but according to studies, people who make natural eye contact are often viewed by people as possessing lots of positive traits, such as emotional stability, confidence, competency, sincerity, honesty, and personal warmth.

This should not be a surprise because when you take the time to truly look at somebody in the eyes in a non-threatening and a non-dominating way, but out of a sincere effort to truly get that person, they can't help but embrace you back at some level or another. Eye contact is a gateway to interpersonal intimacy.

It's the difference between talking to someone and seeing their eyes scan the room behind you (how belittling does that feel?) and someone looking you in the eye and truly engaging.

This power of eye contact cannot be underestimated, and charismatic people simply get to an intimate and personal level with everyone in record time.

Nodding is easy, right?

Simply looking somebody in the eye opens the door to deeper levels of intimacy. However, it cannot exist in a vacuum.

A charismatic presence is the result of a combination of a wide range of consistent signals that you project.

One of the most obvious signals you can send out is to simply nod your head. This means that you are present and soaking things up. This means that you are paying attention to what they are saying. This also means that you are processing the information that they are giving you, and making a statement based on that synthesis.

A lot of people are so eager to please the person that they're talking to that they simply nod a lot. They look like bobble-heads. Instead of somebody that your audience can look at as some sort of credible and authoritative figure, you look like a weak, shallow individual who has an agenda.

The secret here is to nod or send listening signals at appropriate times. In other words, if you are truly listening, you would know that there are logical spaces in the conversation where a nod of approval or some sort of confirmation is not only welcome, but quite necessary. On a subconscious level, the person you're communicating with knows this. When you nod at the right time, they know that you and they are on the same page. That's how you deepen intimacy. You don't deepen intimacy by nodding a lot and simply acting like you're too eager to please them.

Another great signal is simply to put away your phone and resist pulling it out until you have a bathroom break. It's surprising how many of our daily conversations are interrupted by our phones, and it's not something you truly realize until you make an effort to take notice. Phone-free zone!

Clarifying questions.

This is one of the easiest ways to show people that you are actually on their level, or at least attempting to be. Ask questions that clarify what the other person was talking about, and it instantly shows that you are engaged in the conversation and care about its outcome. This is easily the step that most people don't do in normal conversation. It's a great social skill to develop on your way to becoming a charisma powerhouse.

Here are some examples of questions that show that you are really listening and present.

Really?

Why did you think that was?

It sounds like you're saying...

Can you clarify that for me?

So for example...

So you're saying...

Can you tell me more about that?

See how all of these clarifying questions don't even require much work on your part, yet compel the other person to speak? Heck, most of the questions just involve your repeating what they say to make them elaborate on it!

Practicing and mastering clarifying questions is a big step in appearing present because of how it causes someone to perceive you. Unfortunately, if you're trying to think of your next clarifying question while the other person is talking, they will quickly notice that you haven't paid attention to them at all.

Being present, or at least appearing that you are fully present and invested in your conversation partner, will make them feel incredibly special and valued. This is doubly true when combined with the other two main charisma components. Sufficed to say, imparting a feeling of importance on others is key to charisma.

Chapter 3. Powerful charisma needs... power.

Charisma isn't just predicated on being present and paying full attention to someone.

Being present is the gatekeeper for what it takes.

That's where power comes into play for charisma. It's as simple as the following: do you feel more special when someone powerful is focused on you, or when the busboy or barista is focused on you? Do you yourself feel more important when the chancellor of your school commends you, or the janitor?

Power alone may be able to override the other aspects of charisma temporarily, as we see with gold-diggers across the world. (A gold-digger is someone that is dating a rich person solely for their money and power.)

The amount of power we perceive someone to have plays a huge part in their charisma, but that doesn't mean that you're out of luck if you aren't actually powerful. Power comes in many forms and can be defined in even more ways.

When we're dealing with interpersonal interaction, there are different contexts and circumstances. What may be power on one context may actually be weakness or ambiguity in another context.

The most basic view of power is that you have the clear ability to alter the world to your favor. Again, does Bill Clinton or a busboy have more ability to alter the world?

Power doesn't have to be financial in nature.

You don't have to actually have a million dollars in the bank for people to perceive you as powerful. As long as they perceive you as some sort of person with the ability to make things happen that would normally require sums of money, that's power.

You don't have to be built like the Austrian Oak (Arnold Schwarzenegger) to give people the impression that you are physically powerful, as long as people perceive you to have the ability to take care of things that would normally require feats of strength.

Perceptions of power are exactly that, perceptions. And whenever we're talking about perceptions, it's not what you actually have, but what people around you think you have.

The good news is that you only need to appeal to their perception to maintain it. This is the secret of social perceptions of power. People will gladly project power onto you.

Now that we've established that power is situational and reality created by people around you, how do you boost your personal power?

Internal confidence.

For people to project power onto you, you have to radiate certain signals. That's their cue to see you as powerful.

One of the clearest and unmistakable signal of power is confidence.

Where does confidence come from? It's not your last name. It's not how much money you have in the bank. It's not who your parents are.

Many research studies say that the core of confidence is mastery. Being good at something.

Everyone has something that they are the best in the world at. Take a moment to shed your modesty filter and think about what you're objectively better than most people at. What were the steps of hard work to get there?

Regardless of what you're good at, you likely went through a difficult process to arrive at your state of mastery and expertise.

This is the raw ingredient that your mind needs to achieve a state of confidence. You have to find that element in your personal life where you went through some sort of process or you powered through a particularly long and drawn out experience and allow yourself to feel a sense of mastery.

Mastery is the raw ingredient of confidence. You cannot feel confident if you don't feel that there was something that you did or you went through that led to a sense of mastery, which then justifies your confidence.

Dig deep and ask yourself what processes you've been through to improve yourself and enrich your life. They haven't been easy, and yet there you are. This alone is cause for massive confidence because most people haven't done it. Confidence begets charismatic power.

Breadth of knowledge.

Another component of building your charismatic power component is your knowledge base. Again, you are sending out signals that act as cues for people to read power into you.

The more you know, the more powerful you appear. So why breadth of knowledge over deep expertise in one domain?

First of all, it's easier to gain a breadth of knowledge.

A lot of people think that breadth of knowledge means that you have to be some sort of trivia show-winning whiz who knows everything. You don't have to know everything. Instead, you only need to know **enough** about a wide range of subjects.

It's okay to have knowledge that is a mile wide but an inch deep.

Interestingly enough, this type of knowledge may make have people think that you are an expert, even though it's the complete opposite of the traditional definition of an expert.

The fact is that a breadth of knowledge makes you appear intelligent, worldly, educated, read, well traveled... you name it. All of that contributes to a sense of power about you. It also allows you to connect with people in some way on the vast majority of their interests.

Here's the thing with real, focused expertise: people aren't going to relate to you if your academic and intellectual specialty is so specific and so focused that they simply can't get to your mindspace. Sometimes, it's essentially a big "who cares" to them if you're a deep expert.

On the other hand, if your knowledge is so spread out that it impacts all sorts of interest areas, then people, regardless of their interest, can find common ground with you. They look at your knowledge as worldly. They feel that what you know impacts and informs the world in a practical way.

Realistically, people are not going to respect the person who is an expert on soil and worms, versus the person who has a wide breadth of knowledge that knows something about everyone's favorite hobby.

This makes people feel that they learn something new when they talk to you, it's a big part of why we all viewed our teachers and professors as so powerful when we were younger. You're engaged in seemingly intelligent conversation where you are simply bouncing around the ideas that the people you're talking to already have.

You can look very intelligent and powerful if you simply know how to ask the right questions along with that breadth of knowledge.

<u>Control your where.</u>

If you're familiar with the physical and figurative settings of your conversations, this leads to a profound sense of personal confidence and this is reflected in your overall presentation. Think the difference between engaging someone in your backyard versus engaging someone in a foreign country that you know nothing about. This can't help but bubble up to the surface in the form of charismatic power.

The fact that you are so in control and so at ease in your environment triggers them to ascribe power to you. This is why it's a good idea that if you're going to find yourself giving a talk or a presentation in an unfamiliar place, visit that venue at least once to get acclimated. If you're going to a party, get there early and familiarize yourself with the entire area.

Figure out where everything is. Find your bearing. Maybe in your mind, rehearse the things that you're going to be doing. This familiarity can all help build your inner confidence up to a point that people would readily ascribe power and confidence to you.

Make any interaction or encounter less unfamiliar and more predictable so that you can focus your attention on the present, and projecting charismatic power.

You can also change the environment itself to show a sense of power.

Whether it's a ritual or habit, making simple changes to one's environment denotes a sense of power. It says that you're not intimidated, will actively change and affect your environment, and essentially that you'll do what you want, whenever you want.

Move chairs and tables around. Make a setup your own. Move locations. Insist on moving around if you want. Sit or stand where you're not supposed to. Suggest that you walk and talk with someone. Put your feet up. Be completely relaxed and comfortable in your environment.

This triggers a reservoir of confidence because this physical power means that you can make things happen that you can physically see. Moving things around is easy to see. People ascribe power to you because of that sense of calm, confidence, and competency they see you project. And all it took was a small physical ritual of just simply moving things around or asking people to move things around.

Make your words count.

Another key signal people often ascribe power to is the volume, speed, and quantity of your speech.

People who are weak and insecure tend to feel compelled to interact with their environment by throwing spaghetti at the wall verbally. In other words, they keep chattering and chattering in an attempt to captivate people's attention. It seems like literally every sentence is a Hail Mary from these people. After a while it starts to reek of desperation.

The opposite of this is somebody who speaks very little, but when they do speak, they speak slowly and in a measured manner. You aren't out to impress anyone, and don't act like it.

In the same vein, don't scramble to fill silences that you feel might be awkward. People that become uncomfortable with natural conversation lulls and silences are usually too anxious about appearing smart in front of the other person. That's not you.

The subconscious meaning of these actions is that your words count. You're not the type of person who is going to open their mouth to try to placate others or put on a show. When you speak, something will happen. When you speak, you speak with power. Speaking slowly tends to amplify this effect, and people tend to listen.

It's one of the easiest ways you can project power. But it works best with a deep reservoir of confidence. Speaking less and speaking slowly, in and of itself, is not going to trigger projections of power unless it's paired with outer manifestations of deep confidence.

Chapter 4. Warmth and empathy.

The third element of charisma is warmth.

Possessing warm is when people feel that you are approachable, caring, empathetic, and non-judgmental. You care about them, and they feel better about your overall presence. They want to be around you. They feel comfortable and at ease when you're with them.

Since most people do not have this type of warmth, at least when dealing with strangers, it's very easy to stand out if you develop an outward projection that focuses on your ability for empathy.

You have to remember that whenever we're talking about the elements of charisma, we're talking about the projections of people around you. Presence and power can be simulated and impersonated initially, but warmth is the charisma component that is almost impossible to fake.

The easiest way to project warmth is to actually care about people – easier said than done.

So how do you develop this inner core that would result in you externally projecting warmth? Develop your empathy.

Empathy is all about putting yourself in the shoes of other people.

Whenever you say something, think of how it's received by the person you're saying it to. If you want to be perceived as warm, look through the eyes and ears of the person you're talking to. What do you think that person would need to hear for him to perceive you as warm?

Empathy isn't easy because humans are self-absorbed beings. If you strip the human condition of all societal pretense, it all boils down to selfishness.

You have to constantly put yourself out there and really look at how people are going through their lives. Imagine yourself perceiving what they're perceiving, feeling what they're feeling, and really draw your heart closer to them.

One of the most practical ways you can do this is to simply look at people as blood relatives. Just as you would care about a little brother and a little sister, develop a way of caring for other people like they're members of your family. You might not care if a school acquaintance loses their job or wins the lottery, but what if you replace that acquaintance with your mother?

You might be surprised as to how quickly your sense of empathy grows if you assume some sort of genetic and familial connection with people around you. It's tough to not be warm and automatically care in this frame.

<u>See people more.</u>

Another simple and powerful way to boost your empathy level is to simply deal with people on a face-to-face basis as much as possible. I know this might seem dated in the age of Facebook and Skype, but let's keep convenience out of this.

Keep in mind that you're actually missing out on a lot of interpersonal social signals when you simply communicate with people through a screen. A smiley face doesn't really tell the whole story, does it?

Whether it's your tablet, your phone, or your laptop, there's something missing when you communicate with people through online communications. The soul of interpersonal connections is stripped naked. When you deal with somebody on a face-to-face basis, you get a 3-dimensional reading and surround sound perception of their tone of voice, their demeanor, their facial expression, and their personal aura.

It's almost impossible to detect all these signals through a screen. And this is why, according to recent studies, contemporary college studies have 40% less empathy than their counterparts thirty years ago. It's easy to see why. Thirty years ago, there was no Internet, Facebook, FaceTime, Skype, instant messenger, you name it.

If you want to become charismatic and project sincere warmth, you need to put yourself in situations where you can practice empathy. One of the simplest and most powerful ways to do that is to simply engage with people on a face-to-face basis.

Pick up the phone instead of texting. Make plans solely to see people and to catch up more frequently. Practice this sense of empathy and see your charismatic warmth grow.

Other empathy methods.

Another truly effective way to boost your empathy levels is to read more fiction.

Here's the way fiction works. Feelings are never outright said. They are described in detail, and we encounter many situations that cause our protagonist distress or joy. But the feelings are never named, so how do we know what they are feeling? Well, we learn by their subsequent actions and thoughts.

Fiction is all about getting into the heads of characters.

If you read fiction literature, it becomes second nature to you to want to get into the heads of people you read about.

This is very easy to translate to people you talk to. Your first instinct would be to get into their feelings and look at situations from their perspective, and you've literally had experience with what they are probably thinking from the characters that you've read about.

Another approach to building empathy is to develop a different narrative of people who normally annoy or anger you. It's easy to get annoyed or angry at somebody if you're looking at that person purely from your perspective and how you are affected.

It's easy to write people off as simply being jerks because they were mean to you. However, if you read some sort of story into their lives or some sort of explanation as to why they act the way they do, you'd be surprised as to how empathetic you would feel.

One of the most common ways to do this is to look at that schoolyard bully and read into his story an abusive childhood.

Maybe he was lonely when he was growing up, and this is the only way he can establish some sort of power over his life. Of course, it's anybody's guess whether this is real or not. What matters is that you are able to read in a sympathetic story. This can help you develop a deep and profound sense of empathy.

If you are able to step into the shoes of people you'd rather knock out, beat up, or dismiss, then this would enable you to become warmer to people who treat you well.

Finally, you can boost your overall levels of empathy is to simply be curious about people.

You have to remember that life is not all about you, yet you love to focus on yourself. Well, so do other people! They love to focus on themselves and thus talk about themselves to others. Be curious about what you can discover about others and learn from them. Be curious about why they do the things they do, and why. Curiosity is a highly undervalued skill because of the value it makes other people feel.

Once you make that intellectual leap, all sorts of personal changes become possible. Step out of your own head, and look at the world based on what's important to others.

Chapter 5. Charismatic leading.

If you can embody the three charisma components I dove into in the prior chapters, you will automatically be looked at as a leader. There's no way that the charisma you display won't draw people to you, and make them want to follow your actions. That's why it's important to now dive into charismatic leading and how exactly it works best - because you will find yourself in this position.

In reality, most people are looking to be led. Most people would like to think that they are independent thinkers and that they value freedom, but they actually want freedom from choice instead of freedom of choice. In every company and even friend group and social circle, most people are natural followers, while others are constantly looked at to make decisions. You just need to look at how they actually behave instead of what they say.

People want to be led, but they can be very choosy and picky about their leaders. The best leaders are invariably charismatic to a high degree.

You can be called a leader in your job description and follow a checklist of what you think a leader should do, but rarely has that approach produced any leaders of note.

Real leaders don't need titles. Real leaders don't need to look at their names in the hierarchy chart. They simply become leaders because people thrust them towards it.

Deng Xiaoping of China is an extraordinary example of this.

For many years before he died, Deng Xiaoping didn't have an official title. He didn't need one. All the other communist party figureheads had important and fancy titles, and were them administrators and ministers of this or that. But everybody and their dogs knew in China that all power emanated from, and was centralized in one man, Deng Xiaoping. That's the power of charisma.

Charismatic leading is all about leading people through inspiration, rather than through fear or intimidation. Niccolo Machiavelli was a political strategist and theorist who said that it is better to be feared than loved. Charismatic leaders, on the other hand, are loved. They may have very cold-blooded motivations. They may have very calculated agendas. But their source of power is through love and proactive aspiration, instead of fear and reaction.

People who lead through fear basically get people to do things because their followers are made to feel that their backs are against the wall, that if they don't do something, they will suffer greatly. For example, being put to death. It's easy to see how motivating that can be.

Charismatic leaders work from the opposite direction. They

bring out the best in people because all people aspire for something higher than themselves. They look at an external goal that everybody can agree on and work towards, and are more similar to father figures that you don't want to disappoint.

They are able to do this because they show confidence in a vision. And this vision is embodied in how they do things. People look at them and they see a bright future. They see a clear path from difficult Point A to a glorious and bright Point B. This can't help but inspire admiration from people. They lead through example.

Most of us feel that we live in a reality we didn't choose. When we come across somebody who inspires us to rise above the limitations that we set for ourselves, we can't help but feel inspired.

This is why charismatic leaders are so powerful. They don't need force. They don't need guns pointed at people to get them to do what they want them to do. Instead, they let people believe in their inner angels. They let people reawaken to the dreams that they are capable of having.

If the leader is so confident in his vision, this self-belief is so compelling that it just ends up drawing people in. Be that leader and use the three components outlined previously to create that leadership appeal.

A famous psychologist actually identified six different types of leadership, and though all of them require charisma, one type called the affiliative leader fits the mold of leading solely through charisma.

The affiliative leader.

The affiliative leader is somebody who focuses on harmony. This is a person who tries to get all team members or friends more deeply connected with each other. The hope is that once these connections are made, people would collaborate because they have become emotionally invested in their connections. This person works primarily to get people to open up instead of necessarily getting stuff done.

When performed badly, this leadership method doesn't get to the bottom of things. You have to remember that when you're building emotional networks and you're trying to build connections among people, you have to deal with distressing situations like negative feedback. You simply cannot avoid them. You need to look at them straight in the eye.

Unfortunately, bad implementations of the affiliative leader approach focuses so much on making people feel good that negative yet crucial feedback is often swept under the rug. People are often given the wrong impression that the key to solving issues is to constantly talk and talk about it. This can lead to serious problems down the road. At the very least, you can turn a lot of your friends into annoying whiners with this emotional leadership technique.

The best use of the affiliative leader approach is to pair it with a visionary style leadership. In other words, lay out a grand vision and then work on building emotional connections. The secret to success is to get people emotionally invested in the grand vision for the team.

The affiliative leader approach works well if you're trying to patch things up with friends. If your friendship went through a rough spot and people got mad at each other, this emotional leadership approach is a great way of healing rifts and getting the team united so that they can successfully survive stressful situations.

Chapter 6: Who's your charismatic role model?

I make no secret of the fact that I still idolize Will Smith's Fresh Prince character from the similarly named television show, *The Fresh Prince of Bel Air*.

To me, he's everything that a charming, charismatic personality should be. He says what he wants, is amazingly likeable, is comfortable being at the center of the room, is confident to the point of being arrogant, and most of all he is hilarious. He also leads and gets away with far more than he should be able to simply on account of his charisma.

When I was first starting to diligently grow my own charisma quotient and break out of my shell, he was an important concept for me. Since he embodied many of the things I wanted, I was able to grow, sometimes in a forced and artificial way, closer to my personal ideal simply by asking myself one question.

What would the Fresh Prince do?

It's a powerful question to ask yourself for a reasons.

First, it takes the focus off the situation at hand that you might not be comfortable in.

Asking yourself a question about how someone else would act takes the pressure off of asking how you yourself should act. It's always easier to observe and give advice to other people (hello, relationships), and it's no different here. Viewing things through an objective, relatively impersonal perspective and frame of someone else will allow you to analyze the social situation that you are in, and calibrate your next moves.

Second, it allows you to actually develop your charisma to the end goal that you want.

Every time you ask yourself this question, your reaction and justification will become that much easier until it is second nature. There's no awkward fumbling about and analyzing social situations in hindsight – you will essentially be able to condition yourself in the heat of the moment to act how you want and make your actions as a reflex.

Third, simply having a role model (or 3) in mind allows you to analyze what traits you actually value and want to develop.

For instance, perhaps you want to develop more confidence and being more outspoken in social situations. In that case, you might ask yourself what someone like Robert Downey Jr. would do, or whoever the female equivalent might be. For another trait you want to develop, for example a razor sharp sense of wit and humor, perhaps you could ask yourself what Conan O'Brien would do.

Everyone has different strengths and weaknesses, and has a different conception of how they want to be perceived. Not everyone fits the blatantly outgoing mold of being magnetic, and that's fine.

Other people that tend to resonate with others in terms of wanting to emulate: Tyler Durden, Don Draper, Charles Xavier, Jack Donaghy, Ari Gold, John Wayne, Sheryl Sandberg, Jennifer Lawrence, Michelle Obama, Hilary Clinton, Sarah Silverman, Tina Fey... the list goes on. It's about choosing someone that excels in areas that you feel like you don't, and embodying them from time to time to create lasting habits.

Fourth, thinking about what someone would do is like wearing a mask at first. As any trick or treater can attest to, masks empower us and allow us to say and think things that we wouldn't dare to otherwise. In a sense, this becomes a safe place for you to retreat you when you are in an unfamiliar social situation.

This principle is simply about introspection — recognizing your faults and shortcomings honestly, and implementing a quick mental fix to help you develop your skills into a level of magnetism.

What would the Fresh Prince do here? I like to think he would take advantage and do the same!

Chapter 7. Give without receiving.

Human beings are nothing but naked, hairless apes.

When you compare human and chimp behavior, there's not much difference in what motivates us and makes us act. This should not be a surprise because chimps share 98.6% of our DNA.

Regardless of whether evolution is something that informs your worldview, it is undeniable that we are intimately similar. Chimps demonstrate some of the best and worst traits of humanity.

Our behavior stems from primate behavioral patterns, and studies have shown one of the most powerful ways primates build alliances is gift giving. Gifts given purely on their own accord and free will, without the expectation of reciprocation.

And when chimps are kind to other chimps, those chimps always reciprocate. It's primal instinct.

If you want to be perceived as charismatic, you have to be

gracious and tap into this hardwired behavioral pattern. This means you have to be generous with your resources and your time, and give not even considering that you may get reciprocation.

This builds an incredible charismatic goodwill that will have others scrambling to pay you back.

The good news is that this doesn't have to involve money, though it can. This doesn't have to involve tangible goods, though it can. You don't have to go around giving candy bars to everyone you meet.

You can focus on the giving the gift of your emotional support.

We live in such an alienated and busy culture that the simple act of genuinely smiling at somebody is quite rare on a day-to-day basis.

If you are very liberal with the emotional openness and support you give out, this is good enough for people to feel you're being generous. For example, when you show genuine happiness at seeing someone or compliment someone. And when you are generous, they can't help but reciprocate because it's hardwired into the primate brain.

More often than not, people catch onto these gifts that you are bestowing upon them and will seek to reciprocate. If they do, that's just an added bonus to the charismatic presence that you are cultivating. The mindset of genuinely helping others where it may not benefit you is invaluable.

Think of the last time you felt grateful to somebody. It was very hard for you to feel anger or animosity at that person. Why? You were grateful. You were probably in a place where it was easier for that person to persuade you. You were probably in a place where it was easier for that person to develop a strong personal connection with you.

Reciprocity is the ultimate expression of the concept of karma. Karma is the concept that the world works on a singular economy, and that for every good deed you perform, you will receive one from others. Accordingly, if you perform only bad deeds, your luck will be terrible in life.

Simply believe in the ultimate power of karma, and stay generous knowing that even if there is no reciprocation from the person in question, there will be from someone or something else.

Never underestimate the power of reciprocity and generosity.

Of course, you have to make sure that when you are kind and generous to people, you don't send mixed signals of ulterior motives. The second that anyone gets a whiff that you are doing something for your personal gain and not being forthcoming about it, there goes all the goodwill that you have built towards your charismatic presence. Instead, it becomes more about how you are a manipulative user.

When you're around charismatic people and they're projecting all these free emotional goodies, you can't help but walk away thinking, "Wow! I wish I could be like that!"

Charismatic people have often been helped by the generosity of others before them, so it makes sense for them to pass it on, even if there is nothing in it for them directly or immediately. The benefit isn't tangible, but it will come.

Generosity is ultimately charismatic because people feel that you're a good person with nothing to hide, and what they see if what they get. That makes people comfortable, and it doesn't hurt that you're always doing your best to help them!

Chapter 8. Comfort with discomfort.

Charismatic people are simply unflappable. It seems like they've never had a bad day in their lives.

Of course that's not true, but they are comfortable with being uncomfortable. They know it's an inevitable part of life, and are able to brush it off as such. They have perspective on life and never allow themselves to be down for long.

It is very hard to throw them off track. Awkward situations, different people and uncomfortable situations do not faze them the way that they do other people, and we see this as a huge strength.

Your ability to not let small stuff throw you off is part of your overall charisma. It's inspiring, gives others something to live up to, and drags up the moods of others around you.

People cannot help but like people who operate like lighthouses in any kind of foggy situation.

Since it is very hard to get under the skin of charismatic

people, they function like social anchors. They have a very steadying presence and people are drawn to this. They feel that as long as they hang out with these people, they can weather an otherwise uncomfortable and awkward situation. *Everything will be okay.*

This dynamic makes charismatic people even more attractive. Their reliability in all sorts of otherwise stormy and unsettling social situations make people around them seek them out. As I've stated, people are looking for cues on who to take guidance from.

This is why they love charismatic people — when you see somebody retain their composure in an otherwise awkward situation, you cannot help but be inspired. Charismatic people are even keeled and always know what to do and what to say. It does not matter what is happening around them.

In essence, charismatic people appear bulletproof, and this has a very settling and attractive effect on people that they are with.

Instead of getting emotionally caught up in an otherwise trying situation, people cannot help but seek out these charismatic people because they feel that they get a shelter from the storm when they hang out with these people. Moreover, charismatic people know how to work with negative situations. They do not only know what to say so they can diffuse tension, but they actually know the right way to get on people's good side so they can turn a situation around.

You know you are not dealing with a charismatic person when they actually end up throwing gasoline on the fire instead of an already unpleasant situation winding down and everybody going their own way. Uncharismatic people actually make matters worse. They simply say the wrong things at the wrong time or they try to project dominance and this sets people off.

Charismatic people, on the other hand, have a knack of turning bad situations into pleasant ones. This might be because charismatic people don't feel like they have anything to prove to anyone, and they can just focus on improving a situation without protecting their pride or ego. There's a deeper confidence and security at play there.

In fact, truly charismatic people can turn even the worst situation into something inspiring. They look on the brighter side of life because there's simply no use in not. We can only deal with the hand life deals us. In the hands of a charismatic person, even a horrid hand can be inspirational. They break the tension with humor, or a lighter-hearted approach to things.

Charismatic people refuse to be swept by negative emotion. They refuse to take bad events lying down. They always have a way of trying to turn things around or, at the very least, making an otherwise negative experience turn into a neutral experience.

For all these reasons, people flock to charismatic people. They see an alternative way to deal with the negative situations that life often throws our way, and are drawn to the one who makes it happen.

The perspective and mindset is simple. Tragedy X happens to you. But tragedy X, Y, and Z happens to other people on a daily basis, often all to the same person. Your life isn't so bad, is it?

Chapter 9. Make 'em feel special.

Regardless of whether you are drawn to politicians yourself, there is a reason they have so much appeal to literally millions of people.

If you look at the things they say and the things they do, it's clear that they are elected because they make their constituencies feel special.

There is something about the way a politician connects with their concerns that makes them feel validated, heard, and valued. The politician might never have actually met of any his voters, but he has a way of connecting with them emotionally to make them react with him. It's an essential aspect of charisma. They shine a spotlight on the concerns and thoughts of others.

Charismatic people have an organizing, comforting and soothing presence. It is very easy for you to see yourself in their lives and to bask in the confidence, warmth and sense of possibility that they project. They make you feel good about yourself because of their presence, and how they interact with you.

<u>They shine the spotlight on others.</u>

A spotlight is the center of attention, or focus of a conversation.

Truly charismatic people are never that interested in grabbing the spotlight for themselves. Instead, they are very generous with the spotlight. They shine the spotlight on people around them and this makes them even more attractive.

They want to throw parties for everyone else, and are never so interested in celebrating themselves.

They allow others to take center stage, take praise, garner credit, and be the heroes in stories. Make it clear just how important others are you to, or how instrumental they are in making something happen. Praise flows effortlessly from a charismatic person's lips, which ignites an atmosphere of positivity.

Make sure others are aware of your appreciation.

By shining the spotlight on the people you are talking to, it shows that these people matter, and that they are interested in boosting them. Make yourself a beacon of positivity and good feelings.

A successful spotlight will result in someone just wanting you around more because you always bring up stories that make someone look like a stud.

When charismatic people praise and compliment certain elements about the people that they are dealing with, they drive this strong personal connection to a much deeper level.

It also boosts the confidence and presence of the person who is basking in the spotlight. If they were unsure of how confident they should be with their new haircut or their new job, you've just made the decision for them: very!

This is very hard to fake, and there is a sense of genuineness when charismatic people simply wrap their minds in their presence around what is important.

When they are in a crowd, they make the crowd feel special because every person in that crowd feels that the charismatic person is speaking is speaking to them directly. If you were to reduce the crowd dynamic regarding charismatic people, you can get it down to one factor: They know how to make people feel good by speaking to their desires.

Most importantly, they know how to make people feel good in a natural way. You do not get the sense that they are trying too hard or are transparent.

It might seem understated, but the end effect is that they make people's day. They make people feel gratified for having been in their presence. This is a very addictive interplay that draws even more people to charismatic individuals.

Finally, it actually makes the charismatic person appear

more positive and confident, as it becomes evident that they don't feel the need to hog the spotlight or take credit for their ego's sake. It doesn't hurt that you come off as humble and grounded as well.

Just think about how you'd feel if every time you hung out in a group of people, one of those people always brought up stories that made you seem interesting, engaging, and like a superhero? Not a bad way to make an impression, directly and expertly assisted by someone who understands what makes people tick.

All you need to do is treat everyone like it's their birthday every day — make them feel special by letting them feel good about themselves.

Chapter 10. Charismatic people are supporting actors.

Supporting actors have one job in any movie or television show – to make the main actor look good.

If they're not making them look good, they are acting as a foil for the main actor to display a range of emotion, from anger to sadness to joy. It's probably somewhere in a supporting actor's contract that they simply can't outshine the lead actor!

It's the supporting actor who can look devious or evil for a bit, which just emphasizes the lead actor's virtues.

Charismatic people are like supporting actors in many ways. They don't worry about their own glory or pride, and have no problem letting other people shine. They have no issues with their own vulnerabilities and readily admit to them, yet never emphasize weaknesses of other people.

This is attractive for a number of reasons.

We do not like perfection. It's intimidating, distant, and

somewhat off-putting. Vulnerable people are relatable people, and it's what makes us approachable and human.

They readily own up to their mistakes and flaws. They do not come off as defensive. They do not look like they are bending over backwards to cover up their shortcomings. They are quite upfront with it and comfortable with their vulnerabilities.

The funny thing about vulnerabilities – the more comfortable you are with them, the more comfortable others will be. They won't feel like they have to walk on eggshells around you.

In fact, many charismatic people embrace self-deprecating humor. This endears them to people because they are approachable. You know that you are a flawed human being. You know that you have your shortcomings. Nothing would draw your affinity more when you see somebody who is otherwise respectable and admirable owning up to their shortcomings and flaws. You cannot help but identify with that person on a deep person-to-person level.

Have you ever been around an overweight person that was uncomfortable with their weight? It probably felt like you couldn't mention anything about eating or food around them.

The bottom line is people like vulnerability.

They equate it with deep and profound sense of emotional honesty instead of trying to pretend that they never make mistakes. Charismatic people become even more charismatic by simply owing up to their errors – beyond likability, this makes them reliable, honest, and trustworthy. This is someone you can go to battle with.

While charismatic people readily admit where they fall short, they never, ever dwell on other people's shortcomings.

An uncharismatic person will always blame other people for things that go wrong. They would come up with all sorts of excuses to try to take the spotlight out of their own shortcomings. This is done out of insecurity and a fear of rejection – a mistaken fear that the only thing you have to offer others is your perfection and performance instead of your personality.

Charismatic people do not play that game. They never address other people's errors. They do not nitpick. They do not criticize. They do not judge. They know that everyone is fighting their own battle internally on some level, and let sleeping dogs lie. Of course, this creates a nice contrast where charismatic people look like they are taking the higher road because they focus on where they screwed up and how to move forward.

They protect their lead actor – the person they are talking to. This obviously has limits, but the vast majority of life's little negative squabbles are unnecessary to shine light onto. Charismatic people realize the bigger picture.

On a subconscious level, this draws even more people to them because instead of feeling that you are being judged or feeling that this person has some sort of superiority complex, you feel that this person is approachable. This person makes the same mistakes as you and is real about it. They might even reach a level of unspoken bonding, if it is clear that the charismatic person is staying silent for the other person's benefit.

Charismatic people do not cover up or make excuses for themselves. They do not justify. They just focus on what is, try to make things better and learn from their errors, and move on. They allow themselves to be flawed supporting actors because they don't feel the need to be the invulnerable lead actor.

Others go out of their way to paint themselves as an ideal version, but fail to realize that it is a red flag for insecurity.

Chapter 11. Everything is half full.

Everyone's got an inner monologue – that little voice in your head that tells you it's a good idea to feed an alligator by hand.

Your inner monologue represents your deepest thoughts and desires without filter. This inevitably leaks out to affect your external world, and this can be good or bad. Some people do try to feed alligators by hand, and suffer the consequences.

Try as you might to suppress certain thoughts or urges, not everything stays internal.

In other words, the results that you get with your life are caused by what you choose to believe in and how you choose to look at yourself.

Your mindset influences your approach, which inevitably influences your actions.

Every step of that chain is different in the mind of a charismatic person and begets the next.

It is a way of thinking positively about your life, possibilities, and relationship with others.

It all starts as a product of will power.

Just as you can will yourself to be miserable, depressed, discouraged and have low self-esteem, you can will the opposite. It boils down to your choices and how you take in information.

Unfortunately, many people do not want to take advantage of the good news. They only see the negative and how things can go wrong. For example, they would rather just assume that charisma is just something that you are born with, and not that you can gain through practice.

Charismatic attitudes focus on positivity in both situations and people. Life is too short to dwell on what you can't change, so focus on what you can.

As long as you understand the charismatic mindset and apply it to your life, you can learn certain approaches that would lead to more positive results in all areas of your life.

For example, if your attitude is that you **have** to go to a meeting, then you have a **problem** on your hands. That phrasing is all about obligation and twisting your arm behind your back.

When your mindset reframes that situation as you **get** to go meet other people with the opportunity to make more money, what do you think the difference is? In the first scenario, you are dealing with compulsion. You are dealing with something that you just need to do.

Most people do not really respond well to obligation. Many people think it is a waste of time. In other words, it is a negative task.

On the other hand, if you look at the phrasing in the second sentence "you **get** to go to meet with other people with the opportunity to make more money," you look at it as an adventure and **privilege**. You look at it as something that you aspire to or you look forward to.

Your word choice reflects your mindset, and if you choose the correct mindset, your vocabulary will change accordingly. It's a bit circular, so try to change both simultaneously.

Pay attention to how you currently phrase things. You will be surprised as to how negative you are, and how much room there is for positivity. Charismatic people always focus on working towards something and aspiring towards something. They do not focus on having to avoid something or looking at things as tasks and hassles.

Another example of this is interviewing job candidates.

You can have the obligation of interviewing people and get behind on your workload.

Or have the privilege of selecting a great person to join your team and help your workload decrease overall. Again, it is all about how you phrase the same set of facts. It reflects either a positive or negative attitude. Charismatic people always look at the cream filling in the great sweet bun of life. They do not focus on the crust or burnt parts. They focus on a positive sense of possibility.

Negative or uncharismatic people often look at life as a series of obligations and hassles.

If you want to be charismatic person, you need to start paying attention to your vocabulary and ultimately picking your mindset. Pick a sense of possibility. Pick a sense of adventure. Look at what you stand to gain instead of the hassles that you need to go through.

It's the ultimate glass-is-half-full mindset, and can make a true difference in your daily happiness.

Chapter 12. Identify and speak other people's language.

According to years of anthropological research, people like others that look like them.

It was a learned survival tactic, and made a lot more sense when you were somewhat more likely to survive if you stuck with humanoid shapes and avoided tiger shapes.

Now that the only jungles most of us live in are concrete jungles, survival is not usually the concern of preferring similarity and familiarity.

Yet the instinct persists, and we can actually take advantage of it when cultivating our sense of charisma.

A key facet of charisma is being able to mirror them, and seeing and capitalizing on similarity is powerful for that. It's what we're instinctually trained to gravitate towards. Be familiar.

Get on someone's level and speak their language — speak how they speak, act how they act, and use the same phrases they do — and you will instantly be more charismatic.

If you can reflect some of these elements subtly, it's inevitable that others will start relating with you more positively and openly. It's like you are their next-door neighbor from their tiny town in Russia - speak some Russian, throw in some local slang, use Russian mannerisms, and you're practically family.

When you can reflect these elements, others will start relating with you more positively. They feel that you get them. They feel that you understand them.

When they see somebody that acts differently from them or is just unfamiliar, they feel that deep down this person simply does not get them because they are in a completely different wavelength. After all, throughout most of history, you were a threat. If you were a member of a northern army and you saw the uniform of a southern army member, disliking unfamiliarity could literally save your life. The way we act often reflects the way we think.

On the other hand, if you conduct yourself in such a way that you talk like them or you have used the same tone of voice and mannerisms, it is easier for them to relate to you because they feel that you are familiar enough to include in their comfort zone.

You are predictable in a good way. They will feel like they

know how you think and how you will act and react.

Mirroring someone and speaking their language makes you more charismatic – remember charisma is a quality that draws people to you, and comfort and rapport do that.

By consciously working towards a level of similarity, you end up looking like a person of goodwill. You are displaying trust and safety. People sense this and they draw you closer. It is easier for them to open up.

It will be easier for them to find you credible. Once people find you credible, then it is only a short skip and a jump away from them trusting you.

As I mentioned earlier, you can mirror their words, their tone of voice, and their mannerisms. Keep in mind that mirroring is not just about reflecting them on a wholesale basis. Instead, it is all about communicating to them that you share similar values and have the potential to connect intimately.

What's to mirror?

You can mirror physical signals, gestures, tics, and mannerisms.

For example, if you notice that someone uses a lot of gestures when talking, you should do the same. Similarly, if you notice that someone's body language involves a lot of leaning and crossing of arms, you should do the same.

You can mirror their verbals – tone of voice, inflection, word choice, slang and vocabulary, emotional intonation, and excitement and energy.

For example, if you notice that someone continually uses certain words and terms that you might use something else for, talk to them in their language. Similarly, if you notice that someone is excited and pumped about something, you should elevate your energy level so they don't feel that you are just bringing them down.

Mirroring is simply getting on someone's level, which breaks down any possible barriers to better communication and connection.

Subtlety is key.

If you are blatant or obvious in the way you mirror people you are talking to, the whole experience can blow up in your face.

Instead of developing instant rapport and fostering deeper levels of intimate communications, you end up repulsing them because it seems like you are mocking them.

You might look like somebody with ulterior motives. It would appear that you are trying to put one over and manipulate them. Neither of these situations is good, so it is really important to not overplay your hand.

You can use easily mirroring to enhance your charisma, but do not overplay it. Of course, this is very hard to do the first time you try. It is something you perfect through practice.

Start subtle. You need to simply pick up on cues and not get carried away. Mirroring adds an additional dimension to charisma that is somewhere between warmth and presence.

Chapter 13. Make 'em feel important.

Making someone feel important is something the charismatic do automatically. They probably don't even realize it – it's just a byproduct of their intense attention, focus, and genuine interest in people.

You might have that same genuine interest in people, but the key is that charismatic people show it loudly. They wear it on their sleeves, have no problem with it, and will make sure that you know about it.

Making someone feel heard, important, and validated is actually very easy. You just need to react to their words with importance.

You cannot be a blank wall and take it all in with no emotional feedback whatsoever. Nothing about that communicates the fact what they are saying is important to you, and there's absolutely no emotional engagement.

People are always editing themselves when they tell stories. Whenever they strike up a conversation, they are actually quite selective regarding the topics that they choose to dwell on. These topics are selected because somehow, someway they matter on one level or the other to the person who is speaking with you. It's something they want to engage on because it made them feel something.

If you just sit there and nod your head like a robot, things are not going to register to them. They'll probably think you are bored and disinterested – the opposite of making them feel important. The facial expressions, reactions, and gestures that you think are conveying a message likely are not.

To boost your charisma and get people to want to talk to you further, you need to react in a big way that gets you on board with them. You need to get emotionally tuned in, and that's what makes them feel important – that you care so much about what they've said that you are affected emotionally.

When you notice that they are getting heated at certain points in the story, get heated, too. Follow them on their emotional journey that they are sharing – every story has a purpose and point, and it's almost always about how they were made to feel. This sends them a clear and unmistakable emotional signal that their feelings matter.

Of course, you should not just communicate with your tone of voice.

You have to use all the tools in your disposal. These are verbal and nonverbal signals. Your facial expression is particularly helpful. You cannot say that you are truly emotionally engaged when your voice communicates excitement, but your face looks like you are about to doze off in calculus class.

Everything about you – your face, your mannerisms and your gestures as well as your tone of voice and what you are saying must line up. It must all lead to the person you are talking to feeling validated, acknowledged and valued. These are the effects that you produce when you react in a very pronounced way.

For example, when you go home and your dog greets you at the door, they wag their tail so much it looks like they are going to have a seizure.

That signal brings home the point that you truly matter to them – you are special and their world!

While you should not overreact like the golden retriever, you should also react in such a way that it is unmistakable. This can be a fine line because you do not want to come off as emotionally fragile that anything would set you off.

What is important here is whatever you are communicating, as far as physical, verbal and aural reactions are concerned, are rooted in sincere and genuine emotions.

Give them a path to feel special.

If you remember a topic that is important to the person that you are talking to and you bring it up, this is a way of you communicating to that person that what is important to them is important to you as well.

In fact, it is so important that you stored it in your long-term memory and accessed your memory banks to bring it up.

Again, the bottom line is to get people to feel the fact that they matter to you, that they are not just a random face in the crowd, that they have special place in your mind.

According to Ralph Waldo Emerson, most people live lives of quiet desperation. In other words, they feel on a deep level that they are insignificant, so if you are that type of person that makes them feel important, makes them feel special and makes them feel that they stand out in the big scheme of life, they cannot help but be drawn to you. They cannot help but ascribe power to you.

Most importantly, once you become charismatic to one person, it is not uncommon for that person to talk about you in such glowing terms that you become charismatic to others. People do not like to live life on a first-hand basis. They would rather go by reputation, which can be beneficial for you.

It is really important to make people feel that they matter. Regardless of where they come from, regardless of their background, regardless of how high they are in the totem pole, make them feel that they matter.

Chapter 14. Breaking (physical) barriers.

People crave touch.

I know this may sound weird, because if you have ever spent time in crowded public transportation, you might have the opposite conclusion.

The truth is touching others communicates a level of intimacy and comfort. It communicates in no uncertain terms that you accept somebody and don't reject them on some level. Of course, that's the same reason we don't want to be touched by random strangers on the subway.

Just as people want to feel like they matter, people also like to feel accepted. They want to feel like they belong. Nothing makes them feel like they are more accepted than when you hug them.

Enter social touching.

If done right, social touching will not creep out members of the opposite sex or members of the same sex. It's just a way to show your charismatic presence.

When you look at charismatic figures throughout history, you will notice that a lot of them press the flesh. They shake hands, hug people, and are at ease physically interacting with others constantly. This is not just for show.

People who are charismatic do not have a tough time socially touching people that they do not know. To them, it is a very powerful signal that they are welcoming of other people. They open up their inner selves and let people in, and others will almost always reciprocate.

They might not be able to articulate it. They might not be able to reduce it to practical wording, but they know inside that they feel better if you've socially touched them. They just understand that when they are touched in a social manner, they are calmed and opened.

Bill Clinton was famous for his two-handed handshake. He would take your right hand, and then clasp the back of it with his left hand. This is a great example of social touching, and how one little act can impart a lot of intimacy and comfort.

In our modern world, acceptance is one of the most highly priced social commodities. Everybody is so focused on their own agenda.

Unfortunately, what gets lost in the mix is the fact that we are all different people and we all need to be accepted. Just as we all need to be made to feel that we matter and we are important, we also need to feel that we are accepted and belong somewhere.

When you see a person reach out and touch people in a socially accepted way, a lot of this personal alienation goes away. Instead, for that fleeting second, a sense of connection is established. People hunger for that.

What's more is you're just a touchy person, and without fail, the touchy people that can read social touching contextually are by far the most engaging people to be around. Being touched just makes you feel literally interacted with and heard.

Learn from your inner circle.

The best way to learn social touching, so you can have a clear idea of what to do and what not to do, is to simply observe friends and relatives. When you are with your family and you hug each other and clap each other on the back, you would see what the stated rules are as well as what goes unsaid. Now, extend that to your circle of friends.

What are common ways to socially touch friends and acquaintances?

Giving them a hug to say hello, high-fiving, grabbing onto their arm to emphasize a point or your emotional reaction to what they said, or playfully push them if they are sarcastic.

All it takes is a hand on the shoulder sometimes to physically feel connected and engage someone.

You would see also that friends touch each other in a certain way. When they touch, whether it is a peck on the cheek or a hug, there are also other signals being sent out. Pay attention to this because subtle differences in context can shine a spotlight on what is socially acceptable and what is awkward. Notably, there are signs being sent to indicate that the touching is 100% platonic, so there are no misunderstandings.

If you want to truly master the art of social touching, never underestimate the lessons your friends and relatives are giving you through the way they normally touch each other socially. You will see certain contexts where social touching makes sense, and how to do it in a subtle yet comfortable manner.

If you are going to hug somebody, there is a proper time for it. People who are socially inept and what we call "creepy" do not get this because they do not see that there is a context to certain external behavior.

When you touch people socially, this physical contact releases hormones that trigger a sense of friendliness and intimacy. If you want people to trust you, you need to get into social touching. If you want people to find you credible sooner rather than later, you need to leverage the power of social touching.

Another way social touching boosts a charisma is that it instantly puts everyone on the same level. Thanks to education, social background, personal experience and simple personal competence, everybody is on unspoken different levels. Not everybody lives in the same part of town. Not everybody drives the same car. Not everybody is looked at the same way by society.

There are many lines that divide us. However, when you engage in social touching, all of that magically seems to go away. It is like we are all put in the same level. This is not an accident. I am talking about the primate brain.

When you are touched, your brain activity lights up. When you look at a CAT scan of your brain, it looks as bright as a Christmas tree. That is how powerful social touching can be. However, to tap that power so it works for you instead of against you, you need to pay attention to small, subtle cues. This will enable you to figure out which types of social touching to engage in. It also clues you in as to when to touch and for how long.

I know that you probably will not hit the ball right out of the park the first time you step up to the plate as far as social touching is concerned. Practice social touching first with your friends and family members. If you drop the ball, the fallout will be practically zero. Gradually expand the circle when you can expertly tell what is acceptable in what context.

Chapter 15. Infectious emotions.

Charismatic people can be a bit of a puzzle if you think about it.

On one hand, you feel like you truly know them because of how comfortable they allow you to be. But on the other (realistic) hand, you probably don't know much about them at all.

They've just acted in a way to make you so comfortable and penetrate your inner circle so you feel a bond like you've known them since childhood. They know much more about you because that's how they've demonstrated charisma.

You don't know them, but you feel like you do because their emotions have been infectious.

Charismatic people are so socially powerful because they end up drawing people around them into their emotional world.

Whatever they are feeling, they can make you feel. They also have the emotional intelligence to know what you are feeling to get on the same page as you. Charismatic people are emotional savants.

If you want to be truly charismatic, you have to get people to subscribe to your emotional world. Just think of all the great leaders in history – people have responded to them because they hit an emotional nerve that forced people to listen and react. Regardless of how much Martin Luther King Jr. accomplished, it's clear that he is remembered as an amazing leader because of how well he connected with his followers.

You have to get them to a place where what matters to you on an emotional level matters to them as well.

How do you get that level of engagement and profound emotional intimacy?

<u>Heart on their sleeves.</u>

Charismatic people express their feelings in a very spontaneous way.

There is a level of genuineness when people do not hold back on expressing what they are feeling inside. They wear their hearts on their sleeves and don't filter what they want to express. There is a filter for tact, but there is still a very direct line from their thoughts to their words.

Many people may think they do this, but charismatic people do so because they are unafraid to open themselves to judgment by others.

They stand out as genuine, spontaneous and real because the other people surrounding them have a tough time with that same level of openness and emotional bravery.

People are grappling with their own level of emotional expression and intensity. We see people that we want to emulate, and an element that we feel is missing from our daily lives.

It's empowering to see someone express themselves as such, and creates an atmosphere of non-judgment for others to feel comfortable in and inhabit. When you put yourself out there first and don't appear to care, others will follow your emotional lead.

<u>Positive psychology.</u>

If you wish to boost your personal charisma, you need to get in touch with your feelings and express them in a spontaneous and genuine way. (This does not give you a license to throw a temper tantrum.)

When people see that you can freely express yourself on an emotional level, they cannot help but feel drawn to you.

When they see somebody who can get emotional, they cannot help but relate because you are essentially encouraging them to voice their own emotional range. They are drawn to you because they relate and want to be associated with someone like that. They might even be a little jealous if you can express something that they always felt too scared or awkward to themselves.

This can become quite contagious because the more you express your feelings, the more the people around you feel liberated regarding their own.

This call and response dynamic is easy to see in political rallies. The more excited the speaker is: the more animated he becomes, and the more he involves the crowd.

There is a lot of purpose and design to those signals. It's how the politician is able to draw people into their emotional world – with passionate, free expression and communicating it.

Somehow, this leads to a personal feeling of intimacy that you really know the politician because he speaks so freely.

Emotional transference.

Emotional transference is literally when the emotion of the speaker or actor is transferred to the audience. Whatever is important to the speaker ultimately becomes important to the audience.

If you have ever watched a religious leader's speeches, you would notice that there is a lot of emotional transference.

The applause gets stronger as the speaker bangs his fist and speaks louder. The emotional urgency of the crowd grows as the speaker uses bigger gestures and stronger language. It usually becomes an electric atmosphere.

This begins with one simple act: the speaker conveying passion and enthusiasm about their feelings in a genuine way. That's the trigger to this chain reaction. It's intoxicating because people have no choice but to buy into a presence that strong. They can't escape it.

In turn, the audience bounces this back to the speaker, which creates an upward spiral of emotional urgency, emotional engagement and a feeling of connection.

This is how crowds get worked up. Whether the speaker is trying to project confidence, strong beliefs or convictions, it does not matter. Emotions are very infectious in the hands of an able charismatic person.

Eventually, things reach a point where people feel that they have no choice but to follow the direction of the emotional interactions set in motion by the charismatic speaker.

If you look at different powerful political charismatic speakers in history, you would see that the most charismatic tend to mix things up. They throw in humor, wit, irony, sadness, indignation, anger, shock, suspense — you name it. But it's still an emotional fireworks show to ensnare you and make you engage.

The good news is you can be that figure. It all begins with you being spontaneous with your emotions, conveying them in ways that others can relate to, and then picking up signals from others.

Instead of dancing with your legs and feet, you are dancing with your emotional openness and bravery, your tone of voice, your facial expression, and the reaction of the crowd.

Seeing what people are feeling and empathizing with them is one matter. But being able to draw people into **your** emotional reality and make them feel your ups and downs is charisma on a different plane.

Chapter 16. Turn charisma on like a light switch.

I don't care how shy you think you are, or how much of a social leper you view yourself as.

There has been at least one time in your life when you feel comfortable and happy being at the center of attention, and where you can make friends with anyone. When you've been in *the charisma zone*.

This chapter is going to walk you through the process of identifying your most charismatic states and how you can turn it on at a moment's notice.

First, we have to remember that your shyness/anxiety/nervousness is only a state of mind... and **states of mind can be consciously and willfully changed** in many ways.

When you dig deep, you'll find that there are certain aspects of your personality that are actually quite charismatic. It's just waiting beneath negativity and anxiety of ""I just don't like small talk," or "I'm just not a social person at parties!" to be summoned and expressed.

The first step in turning on your charismatic self at a moment's notice is to identify the range of your charismatic state. Think about the last time you were pumped up and really in the zone. Now break that emotional state down. What made you feel that way, what was happening, and most importantly, why did you feel that way? Sketch out the broad outlines. Be completely honest with yourself. Get in touch with that emotional state.

What were the external triggers? Did something happen that pushed you into that social state? Was it a word that somebody said? Were you wearing certain clothes that helped you feel really comfortable in your skin? Did you go out with a specific friend?

What aspect of your psychology was fed by these triggers? Was it your need to be appreciated? Was it your need to be validated? Was it your need to conquer or to explore? Identify these and be clear regarding these emotional bases.

The second step in calling up your charismatic self at a moment's notice is to pair physical rituals with the emotional triggers that you isolated earlier.

Certain emotional states can be called up based on our physical state, especially when they are paired together. The body has 100% influence over the mind and what the mind perceives... so you literally make emotional connections between things that are happening physically with what you are feeling at the current moment.

Just think of it as a modern re-imagining of Pavlov's dog. Pavlov's dog began salivating every mealtime, which was accompanied by a ringing bell. Eventually, the dog began to salivate at the sound of any bell because he was conditioned to believe that a bell means that food is coming.

Likewise, you can use an external stimuli call up mental states.

Visualize the emotional triggers that caused your moods, or surround yourself with the external triggers. Perform physical acts like push-ups, jumping up and down, slapping your wrists, breathing deeply, standing on the balls of our feet... anything small and subtle will do. And just like Pavlov's dog, eventually even if the triggers aren't present, you can literally train yourself to get into your desired social state.

After all, what good is having a charismatic side if you can never let it surface?

The reason this is works is that you mimic your physical responses when you're at a peak charisma state. Remember when you were talking to that highly attractive person of the opposite sex, your blood was probably flowing, your adrenaline was pumping...You can replicate that physical state by doing push-ups.

So when you do the push-ups, you can replicate the emotional state as well. The best part is that you can call it up whenever you want.

You can exert a high degree of mastery over your emotional state.

As the old saying goes, "The person who masters himself masters the world."

Chapter 17. Charismatic body over mind.

Clubs are notoriously difficult and uncomfortable environments for most people. It's loud, people are stumbling around drunk, and you can't hope to have any kind of conversation there. (Or maybe I'm just not 21 years old anymore...)

Yet we all have friends that love club-hopping and seem to thrive in that environment. Hell, you can probably throw them into any kind of social situation, and they'll instantly adjust their fluency to fit in perfectly each time.

I'd bet the house that if you asked this person what their secret is, they'd tell you that it's a conscious choice and mindset they make to be social.

It's not something that's always on. It's not something that is in effect by default. It's something that they consciously choose. And they can turn it on and off whenever they want.

How?

When you choose to physically act in a charismatic manner, your mind will follow your decision.

Your external physical actions will inform your mental state of mind.

It's the phenomenon of the attribution theory that is so well studied in human psychology. By simply going through the physical motions of something, your mind will mentally note that you are okay with it... and when you accomplish a charisma victory, it will mentally note that you excel at it. And that's how confidence grows.

So focusing on simply **acting**, regardless of your fears, will trigger internal changes over a short period of time to enhance your charisma.

All we can control as humans are our actions and reactions. You might have a lot of doubt and conflict about your fears, but if you resolve to just go through the motions and process, the results you see externally will translate to your mindset and confidence.

Now that we've established that external action is a necessary precursor for the internal changes... what are the external actions we should master to effect that improvement?

Just stand up straight.

When you look into any social setting or crowd, you will notice that there are certain people that carry themselves a certain way... and it's easy to spot them because of their powerful and confident posture. They're standing at attention with their arms loose at their sides in a position of power.

Don't shrink down into yourself and hunch your shoulders, while retracting your chest. We all know that's a universal signal for discomfort and anxiety.

Put your chin up, puff your chest out, and hold your arms behind you. This is going to feel unnatural and like you're showing off your cleavage at first, but take a look in the mirror and look at how much better you look instantly just by standing up straight.

Deep down those people that stand out in crowds — they might be amazingly unconfident or insecure. But guess what? We can't tell, and we treat them like how we perceive them physically.

When you assume powerful body language, you speak more loudly and project better. Exaggerate your facial expressions. Use bigger and more powerful gestures. Smile confidently and engage others. These are the hallmarks of acting socially fluent, and your mind will believe the physical reality that you've created for yourself.

This might be the most empowering proposition in this book, and that's saying a lot.

If you feel defeated or small inside, you can simply physically project the opposite and *change your reality*. Studies have shown that simply smiling more can improve people's moods exponentially, so imagine how just making the choice to act can help you.

At the most basic levels, **our brains are slaves to our bodies**. This is why so many of our daily decisions defy logic and can even be detrimental for us. However, we can bend it to our advantage in gaining social fluency by forcing the mind to accept certain realities that we physically project for ourselves.

It doesn't happen overnight, but it will happen. The more you go through the motions of social fluency and make the choice to do it, the more you can achieve and alter your internal mental state.

You might not even realize that it's happening until you're suddenly at a party socializing without a care in the world and think "I would not have been able to do this a month ago…!"

The more you practice, the better you get at it, and the better you will be able to feel about yourself **on command**.

Chapter 18. Cultural differences in charisma.

There is a famous saying attributed to Hermann Goering.

He said that whenever he hears the word culture, he reaches for his gun. Culture is very divisive. What works in one cultural context can lead to you going to jail or being beaten up in another culture.

Charisma is one of those elements that can be problematic if we apply a cultural filter... which you always should. You have to always keep this in mind because it's very typical of westerners to believe that bigger is always better. Westerners also often prioritize convenience over other values. This doesn't cut across the board.

In fact, that's the biggest factor to consider when dealing with people of different cultures. Becoming larger than life is a western ideal, where leading by quiet confidence is more likely to be strived for in the east.

Take Japan, for example. In their case, bigger isn't necessarily better. After all, Japanese culture came up with the Zen saying, "Less is more." That is just unbelievable to a typical westerner, who literally feels charismatic by overwhelming a room of people.

No matter where in the world you are, people bring their cultural expectations with them.

When interacting with different ethnic markets or members of the opposite sex from different cultures and different traditions, you have to pay attention to how those cultural differences impact perceptions of charisma.

Charisma is ultimately contextual. It's all about paying attention to the signals being sent by the greater reality around you, and you responding to those signals. If you respond optimally, you are charismatic. If you get your wires crossed, you come off offensive, or even worse, a threat.

Here are just some common problems that take place when people try to be charismatic in different cultural contexts.

Western cultures prioritize bigger.

If you come on strong, you are often perceived as confident. Larger than life, so to speak.

In eastern cultures, if you come on strong, you either come off as somebody who is imposing or somebody who is a social climber. Neither of these situations is good. So it's really important to know where to draw the line. Otherwise, you're going to draw suspicion and skepticism instead of admiration and loyalty.

When projecting power, you are dealing with your confidence level. Your confidence level is the trigger, and the ascription of power is the effect. However, in an eastern context and other cultural contexts, it's too easy to step over the line. Instead of being confident, you come out as cocky and arrogant. In eastern contexts, humility actually draws more ascriptions of power than raw displays of confidence.

In certain cultures, hugging somebody and kissing them, even though you are of the same sex, is a genuine reflection of warmth. People can't help but open their hearts to you because you go through the motions of empirically communicating your warmth and empathy.

In eastern cultures, people are more reserved, and same sex kissing and physical contact sends a completely different set of signals. In fact, any contact of any kind might be over the line in some parts of the world.

Warmth is the most culture-dependent charisma component, as affection and positivity is shown in too many different ways.

Being overly touchy-feely, regardless of cultural context, can often look fake, manipulative, and driven by an ulterior motive. Instead of developing instant rapport and interpersonal intimacy, people can become overly suspicious and skeptical of you.

It should be no surprise that different cultures have different points of emphasis, and even for what's acceptable. An essential part of everyday charisma is tailoring your approach to evoke your most charismatic self in any situation.

Conclusion

Bill Clinton has taught a few lessons in his day, but the most important to me was the learnable nature of charisma.

By breaking the mindset that it was just something that people were born with, it opens up a world of possibilities for anyone seeking to improve themselves. Sure, charisma can appear effortless and at times incredible, but 99.99% of the time it's a product of years of learning and practice.

I'd pay a lot of money to see Bill Clinton at his first public speaking engagement – see what I mean?

Everyone starts somewhere, and power, warmth, and presence are all learnable quantities.

It's my hope that you've taken something that you can instantly put into use from this book, and many longer-term strategies for growth.

As for Bill? Well, it's a miracle that I've gotten through this entire book without making a Monica Lewinsky joke.

Sincerely,

Patrick King
Dating and Social Skills Coach
www.PatrickKingConsulting.com

P.S. If you enjoyed this book, please don't be shy and drop me a line, leave a review, or both! I love reading feedback, and reviews are the lifeblood of Kindle books, so they are always welcome and greatly appreciated.

Other books by Patrick King include:

CHATTER: Small Talk, Charisma, and How to Talk to Anyone

MAGNETIC: How to Impress, Connect, and Influence

Conversationally Speaking: WHAT to Say, WHEN to Say It, and HOW to Never Run Out of Things To Say

Cheat Sheet

Chapter 1. Charisma demystified.

Charisma is a learned quantity, not simply something that some people are born with, and some people are born without. It is essentially the power to draw people to you, and has the power to change your life.

Chapter 2. Living in the here and now.

The first component of charisma is being present, and that is when you focus your attention on the situation and person at hand. You ignore worrying about your future, and what other people are doing. Live in the now because you'll never get it back.

Chapter 3. Power for powerful charisma.

Power is the second component of charisma. Power is doesn't have to be traditional, such as financial or prestigious. As long as you give the impression of power through body language and controlled speech, people will impart power to you and treat you with importance.

Chapter 4. Warmth and empathy.

Warmth is the third component of charisma. Giving people the sense that you are empathetic, warm, and non-judgmental will draw people to you and make them open up to you. You make people feel heard and validated.

Chapter 5. Charismatic leading.

Invariably, the best leaders possess high amounts of charisma that make people simply want to follow them. There is also a type of leadership that fits charisma exactly – the affiliative leader, who leads by harmony and nurturing relationships.

Chapter 6: Who's your charismatic role model?

Sometimes we do best by copying someone. Collect a few mental role models where you can just imagine what they do – this will decrease your mental burden and make clear your charismatic end goal, which is important to know.

Chapter 7. Give without receiving.

Charismatic people make others want to be around them by being generous and giving, without expecting anything in return. Give first, affect people, and reap the rewards down the line. You will become a role model and something for people to aspire to.

Chapter 8. Comfort with discomfort.

Charismatic people are unflappable. They are even keeled and emotionally stable. This is comforting for people, and enforces the charismatic person's position as an emotional leader.

Chapter 9. Make 'em feel special.

Charismatic people shine the spotlight on others, which means that they like to praise others and have them be the focal point. They don't need to protect their pride or ego, and let others be the hero as much as possible.

Chapter 10. Charismatic people are supporting actors.

Charismatic people don't have a problem with their own flaws and vulnerabilities. If they are openly comfortable with them, so are other people. However, they don't nitpick or bring others down, and keep positivity the first priority.

Chapter 11. Everything is half full.

The mindset that allows for mass charisma is one of redirection and reframing. There is a silver lining to everything, and it's a matter of will to find it and focus on it.

Chapter 12. Identify and speak other people's language.

People like similarity, so actively seek to identify someone's language. Their mannerisms, vocabulary, and body language is all something that you can learn to subtly emulate, which will make them more comfortable with you subconsciously and immediately.

Chapter 13. Make 'em feel important.

Don't have a poker face. Show your reaction loudly to people and make them feel heard. This simple acknowledgment is powerful, and makes people feel emotionally validated.

Chapter 14. Breaking (physical) barriers.

Social touching is what family and friends do, so you must learn how to do so in the correct context. This will make people trust you more quickly, and is a key component to drawing people to you.

Chapter 15. Infectious emotions.

Charismatic people have the ability to impart their emotional message to people around them. This is because of how comfortable they are with expressing their emotions spontaneously, which allows others to do the same.

Chapter 16. Turn charisma on like a light switch.

Just like any emotion or mental state, charisma can be triggered if you know what triggers it. Find the triggers, pair them with your charismatic states, and practice until it's like a light switch.

Chapter 17. Charismatic body over mind.

Your body is the boss of your personality. If your force your body to act in ways that a charismatic person does with posture and body language, you can literally summon the mental part.

Chapter 18. Cultural differences in charisma.

The biggest difference in eastern and western views of charisma is the concept of big. In the west, bigger is considered better, where it would be seen as extraneous and arrogant in the east.

42336432R00060

Made in the USA
Middletown, DE
09 April 2017